I work as a Kennels Assistant

by Clare Oliver

Photography by Chris Fairclough

W

FRANKLIN WATTS
LONDON • SYDNEY

© 2001 Franklin Watts

First published in 2001 by
Franklin Watts
96 Leonard Street
London
EC2A 4XD

Franklin Watts Australia
56 O'Riordan Street
Alexandria
NSW 2015

ISBN: 0 7496 4059 6
Dewey Decimal Classification 636.7
A CIP catalogue reference for this book is available
from the British Library

Printed in Malaysia

Editor: Kate Banham
Consultant: Beverley Mathias, REACH
Designer: Joelle Wheelwright
Art Direction: Jason Anscomb
Photography: Chris Fairclough

Acknowledgements
The publishers would like to thank Stuart Nicholls,
Don and Jackie Jeffery and the staff at Briafield
Kennels, Twyford, Berkshire, for their help in the
production of this book.

Contents

(Note: words printed in **bold italics** are explained in the glossary.)

Meet Stuart

Would you like a job working with dogs? That's what Stuart always wanted. For nine years now he has worked at his local **boarding kennels** – a 'hotel' for pets when their owners are on holiday.

At busy times of the year – such as the summer months, or around Christmas and Easter – there may be as many as 50 dogs and 20 cats at the kennels. Looking after them all is hard work, but very rewarding.

Stuart has a pet dog at home.
It is a boxer, called Tyson.

For much of the year, the animals are looked after by just Stuart and his boss, Jackie, and three part-time workers who come in just in the mornings. However, at peak times, Jackie employs up to seven part-time workers. Often, these workers are still at school or college, but their holidays are when the kennels are busiest.

Like many kennels, the one where Stuart works houses cats as well as dogs.

Favourite Five

Stuart's favourite dogs are:

1. Mastiff
2. Boxer
3. Rottweiler
4. Ridgeback
5. Bulldog

JUST THE JOB!

Kennels Assistant

Stuart's job is quite varied. His main *duties* include:

- Preparing and *distributing* the dogs' food
- Washing out the dogs' beds and cages
- Exercising the dogs
- Showing customers around the kennels
- Taking bookings

First Tasks

Work at the kennels starts at 8 a.m. sharp. The first duty of the day is walking the dogs. Jackie tells Stuart and the part-timers which dogs to walk.

Top Tips

Here are Stuart's top dog-walking tips:
- Walk more *aggressive*, highly-strung dogs when there are no other dogs around.
- Sit with an *excitable* dog and talk softly to it until it calms down.
- Let friendly dogs race about off the lead sometimes, to give them a chance to be *sociable*.
- Give the dogs a cuddle, so they don't feel lonely.

Stuart takes the dogs that are most difficult to handle because he is used to putting nervous dogs at their ease. Also, Stuart is at the kennels all day long, so the dogs are more used to him.

It takes Stuart ten minutes to cycle from home to the kennels.

ach person takes out one dog at a time and walks it around the paddock on a lead. No more than six dogs are walked at the same time. This limits the possibility of dogs attacking one another.

Finally, it's time for the walkers' least-favourite task – cleaning up all the dog mess. Stuart hands out the poop-scoopers, and everyone sets to work.

The most difficult dogs are not always the biggest. Small dogs like this West Highland terrier can be quite a handful!

Dog Walkers

The dog-walkers don't just walk the dogs. Their other tasks include helping Stuart with:
- **Poop-scooping**
- **Washing out the dogs' beds and cages**
- **Feeding-time**

Clean-Up Time

Once all the dogs have been walked, it's time to clean out their cages. The workers pair up and Jackie divides the different dog 'houses' between them.

Each cage has two areas. The indoor area is where the bed is; then a dog-sized door leads to an outside run. As each dog comes back from its walk, it is put in the run so that the indoor areas can be cleaned.

First the beds are taken outside and swilled with *disinfectant*, then hosed down with cold water. The sleeping areas are also disinfected. The floor is brushed hard then washed down with a hose.

Stuart mops disinfectant round each bed.

The cleaned beds are left upside down to dry.

Then Stuart and the others have to **coax** the animals into their sleeping areas. When all the dogs are safely inside, each run is hosed down – and the dogs' water bowls are topped up at the same time.

The drain in the centre of the dogs' house carries away the excess water.

Stuart gives each water bowl a thorough scrub with a washing-up brush.

Essential Kit

This is what Stuart wears:
- **Baseball cap** – to keep off the sun, or rain.
- **Long-sleeved sweatshirt** – to protect his arms from scratchy claws.
- **Jeans** – it doesn't matter if these get dirty, and Stuart can clip his keys to the belt loops.
- **Trainers** – Stuart's on his feet all day, so he needs comfortable footwear.

Dogs' Dinner

It's hard work dishing up dinner for 50 dogs! Mostly, the dogs are fed on dry food, which Jackie buys in bulk.

Some dogs are very fussy. Their owners leave special instructions about which foods they eat, and sometimes even leave their pets' favourite snacks with Stuart.

Stuart has a list showing each dog's preferences. When new dogs arrive, their requirements are added to the list.

Stuart checks the list to see if any of the animals need special food or *medication*.

Stuart hides pills inside a dog's food. Then he feeds the dog by hand, so he knows that the pill is eaten.

Tricky Moments

Some dogs get upset tummies at the kennels. These dogs are given special dry food to settle their stomachs. Stuart has to:

- Check the cages for signs of *diarrhoea*.
- Check that the dogs do not refuse to eat two meals in a row.
- Check that the dogs have not been sick after eating.

There are two sizes of food bowls – for large dogs and small dogs. There are also different-sized scoops to ensure that no one overfeeds the dogs. But Stuart has been feeding dogs for so long now that he can measure out the food by eye.

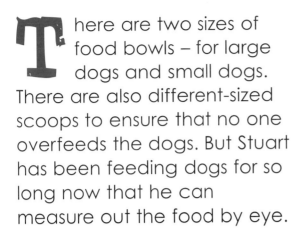

The hungry animals wolf down their meal.

Stuart puts all the dishes in order, so he can remember which food is for which dog.

In and Out

One very important part of Stuart's job is dealing with customers face-to-face. Each morning Jackie leaves two sets of forms in the office – one for animals due in, and another for those leaving.

When owners drop off their pets they sign a form, handing over responsibility for the pet to the kennels.

Stuart checks the forms early in the day so that he knows what to expect. This means that everything runs smoothly when the owners arrive to drop off or pick up their pets.

Stuart has to be sensitive. Some people, especially young children, can get upset when leaving their pet.

14

Stuart listens for customers arriving. He can tell that people are outside before they ring the bell, because all the dogs in the kennels hear the car pull up and start barking even more than usual!

Stuart also shows round would-be customers. At first he was nervous about this, but over the years he has become more confident. When the customer has looked over the kennels, they often want to book a place there and then. Stuart writes down the dates and other details, such as the breed of dog, in the diary. Sometimes he calls for Jackie so that she can make the booking.

▲ When a customer comes to pick up their pet, Stuart finds the dog's lead then collects the dog.

One of the best parts of Stuart's job is *reuniting* a dog with its family. ▶

In the afternoon Stuart and Jackie let out the more sociable dogs in groups of about four. They play in Jackie's garden and the paddock. This allows the dogs to stretch their legs a bit more than in their runs. Stuart checks on them regularly, and clears away any messes they have made.

Stuart cleans out the drains once a week to stop them getting clogged up with dog hairs.

Jack of all Trades

There's more to Stuart's job than looking after the dogs. Some of his other tasks include:
- Counting the cash in the till
- Checking that there is enough food in the food shed
- Cleaning out the drains
- Sweeping the training shed
- Maintaining the buildings
- Mowing the paddock

On quiet days, when there are not many dogs being brought in or picked up, Stuart often has time to spare. He fills the afternoon doing odd jobs around the kennels.

About twice a week, Stuart sweeps out the training shed. Jackie takes some animals here for obedience training.

On late summer afternoons Stuart clears up fallen apples in the paddock.

Stuart uses his spare time in the afternoons to give the buildings a fresh coat of paint.

Being Responsible

Stuart has to be very responsible, because there are living creatures in his care. This means checking on the animals regularly, making sure they have enough water and that they are not too hot or too cold.

Stuart watches out for unusual behaviour. He knows that healthy, happy dogs should be bright-eyed, clean-nosed, and **responsive**.

Stuart reassures animals that can't settle down. This little King Charles spaniel soon responds to special attention.

Throughout the day, Stuart checks on the heaters in the dog houses.

18

No dog is allowed to stay at the kennels unless it has up-to-date *vaccinations*. However, sometimes dogs become sick during their stay, especially if they are old.

Health Check

Stuart looks out for these signs when checking on the dogs:

- Inactivity – when a dog just lies around and doesn't respond
- Diarrhoea
- *Discharge* from the eyes or ears
- Extremely smelly breath
- Constant panting, *irregular* breathing or wheezing

JUST THE JOB!

Vet

Being a vet takes serious training. Some people say it is harder to be a vet than a doctor! Vets learn how to treat lots of different animals, from hamsters to horses.

There are only six universities in the UK that teach animal medicine, so competition is fierce. You need three good science A-Levels, and the courses last at least five years. At the end, a vet can join the Royal College of Veterinary Surgeons and go into practice for him or herself.

Stuart prefers to let Jackie call the vet while he sits with the sick dog. But if Jackie is out, Stuart calls the vet himself.

Grooming Marvellous

Some owners ask for their pets to have a thorough grooming while they're at the kennels. Stuart writes requirements like this in the diary so he doesn't forget.

Janet hoses Poppy down in the grooming parlour's bath. ▶

Poppy is *tethered* to the grooming table while Davina gently blow-dries her fur. ▲

The grooming parlour, called Hair of the Dog, is close to the kennels. Stuart books appointments with Davina, who runs it. The parlour also takes appointments from animals not staying at the kennels. It is so popular that on some days Davina's mum, Janet, comes in to help.

Davina gets rid of any excess fur with a grooming mitt. It leaves Poppy's coat shiny and smooth.

Animal Beautician

Davina knows how to style just about every breed of dog – from poodles to Afghans. You don't need *qualifications* to be a pet beautician, although you can take a City and Guilds qualification in Dog Grooming. Davina learned her trade by working as an assistant at a grooming parlour.

When it's time for their appointment, Stuart takes the dogs to the parlour, and picks them up again at the end. A visit to the grooming parlour can mean a bath and blow-dry, claw-clipping, or even an all-over trim.

Davina clips Poppy's claws to stop her damaging furniture or accidentally hurting people if she jumps up.

Davina uses clippers to give Poppy an all-over trim.

21

Pros ...

W hat Stuart loves most about his job is working with animals. The dogs respond to kindness with great loyalty and affection, and that makes Stuart feel good.

A few years ago Stuart had to go into hospital after an accident, but he was so keen to be back at work that he begged to be allowed to leave hospital early. He believes working at the kennels speeded up his recovery.

This little terrier has to wear a collar to stop it chewing at a torn claw. ▼

◄ Stuart likes to groom the animals staying in the cat 'hotel'.

22

There are lots of other great things about the job, too. Stuart would hate to be cooped up in an office. At the kennels he is outside a lot of the time. And of course, because the kennels are near to Stuart's house, he doesn't have to travel far to get there.

Stuart gets on well with his boss, Jackie. They know each other well now, and like to share a joke.

Don and Jackie live on the _premises_. By law, someone has to be on hand to look after the dogs 24 hours a day.

The atmosphere at the kennels is very friendly. Jackie and her husband, Don, really care about Stuart and he cares about them. Still, a lot of the time Stuart works on his own, and this gives him a sense of independence. Knowing that Don and Jackie trust him has really built up his confidence, too.

O f course, working at the kennels would not suit everyone. Despite starting work at 8 a.m., Stuart sometimes has to come back in the evening if Don and Jackie want a night off. And the days that most people do not work, such as weekends or Christmas, are the times that Stuart cannot take off, because Don and Jackie need him most. That does not leave Stuart much time for a social life.

Poop-scooping is one of the least pleasant tasks that Stuart has to do.

Stuart has to keep an eye on the part-timers, and report any problems to Jackie. Sometimes this can be awkward.

Spending most of the day outside is wonderful in summer, but not so good in winter. It's hard work too, and Stuart is often tired out when he finally goes home. Some of the dogs are dangerous, and Stuart has been bitten several times. Once, he needed stitches.

It is extremely noisy at the kennels, because of the constant barking.

Some of the tasks are quite *strenuous* while others are boring and repetitive. Even so, Stuart would not give up his job for anything.

One of Stuart's tasks is to open and close the windows of the cat hotel, to make sure the cats get enough fresh air.

BRIAFIELD KENNELS
Boarding and Cattery
Dog Training and Agility
TEL 0118 969 0834
OPEN 8.00am - 12.30pm DAILY

After a long, tiring day, Stuart hops on his bike and sets off home.

Finding a Job

The only qualifications for being a kennels assistant are that, like Stuart, you must be healthy and love dogs. Strength and fitness are essential – not just so that you can control the dogs, but also for the manual labour, such as cleaning out.

It helps if you can tell an Alsatian from an Afghan, so read up as much as you can about dog breeds.

> You absolutely have to love animals to do a job like Stuart's – otherwise all those dogs would drive you mad!

Job Know-How

What qualifications do I need?
None. English Language and Maths at GCSE will help with the small amount of paperwork that you need to do.

What personal qualities do I need?
Responsible and reliable. Healthy, energetic and strong. Love of animals.

How do I apply?
Watch the local press for adverts, or contact your nearest kennels direct and ask if they need extra help.

Will there be an interview?
Yes – to check you get on with animals, and also with the other kennels-workers.

You need to get on well with people as you will be dealing directly with customers. You may even have to reassure owners who are calling long-distance from their holidays to check on their pet!

Many schools organise **work experience**, and you could try to be placed at your local kennels, a veterinary practice, or even a pet shop (which is where Stuart started work). A kennels-owner will prefer to employ someone who has experience of working with animals. Even a track record of looking after your own or a neighbour's dog might help.

Jackie knows that she can trust Stuart to lock up properly.

Taking a holiday job at your local kennels is the ideal way to learn about the work hands-on – and find out if it's really the job for you.

Glossary

Aggressive	Violent and likely to attack.
Boarding kennels	A place where dogs, and sometimes cats, are looked after while their owners are on holiday.
Coax	Persuade or tempt.
Diarrhoea	A stomach illness.
Discharge	Gluey liquid that comes out of the eyes or ears.
Disinfectant	Something that kills germs to prevent the spread of disease.
Distributing	Handing out.
Duties	Jobs that must be done.
Excess	Extra, or not needed.
Excitable	Easily excited.
Irregular	Not regular, unevenly spaced.
Medication	Medicine, such as tablets, pills or injections.
Premises	The buildings and grounds that a business occupies.
Qualifications	Official requirements for a particular job.
Responsive	Responding to touch or noise, being alert.
Reuniting	Bringing back together.
Sociable	Enjoys being with others (dogs or people!).
Strenuous	Active, full of effort.
Tethered	Tied to something.
Vaccinations	Injections that prevent disease.
Work experience	An unpaid period of work, often for a week, so that a person can see what a job is like at first-hand.

Find Out More

House your pet at the kennels where Stuart works:
Briafield Kennels
Waingels Road
Lands End, Twyford
Berkshire RG10 0UA

Visit this website to find out the names and addresses of boarding kennels in your area:
www.kenneldirectory.com

Learn more about dog breeds and shows by writing to:
The Kennel Club
1–5 Clarges St, London W1Y 8AB

There are lots of magazines and newspapers specially for people interested in dogs.
Look in your local newsagent for:
Our Dogs
Dog World

Contact this charity to find out about approved kennels:
Royal Society for the Prevention of Cruelty to Animals (RSPCA)
Causeway, Horsham
West Sussex RH12 1HG

In Australia you can contact:
Royal Canine Council Ltd
44 Luddenham Road
Erskine Park, NSW 2759
Check out their website at:
www.rnswcc.org.au

Another website to look at is:
www.dogzonline.com.au

For more information, try this magazine:
National Dog Magazine
Email: natdogs@ozemail.com.au

Also, why don't you…
• Visit your local library and check out the careers section.
• Look in your local library for books about dogs, too.
• Find out if there is a teacher at your school who is an expert careers advisor.
• Look in your local business directory under 'Kennels' to find out who to contact for work experience placements.

Index